I0759798

For my grandchildren, Reese Booker-LaNier and Jalen McClean, so they and other young people might learn from the Little Rock Nine about perseverance in the face of adversity

—CWL

For all our great ancestors and the Little Rock Nine, who came before us to pave the way for us to receive education

—VBN

About This Book

The illustrations for this book were created using Photoshop, Procreate, and the illustrator's own collage papers. This book was edited by Samantha Gentry and designed by Patrick Collins and Saho Fujii. The production was supervised by Nyamekye Waliyaya, and the production editor was Jake Regier. The text was set in Adobe Jenson Pro, and the display type is Arima Koshi.

 The text begins on page 6. Photos from September 4, 1957, and September 25, 1957, on pages 44–45 courtesy of the Will Counts Collection: Indiana University Archives. All other photos on pages 44–45 courtesy of Carlotta Walls LaNier. Photo of Carlotta's diploma on page 47 courtesy of the Collection of the Smithsonian National Museum of African American History and Culture, Gift of Carlotta Walls LaNier. Little, Brown and Company • Hachette Book Group • 1290 Avenue of the Americas, New York, NY 10104 • Visit us at LBYR.com • First Edition: January 2026 • Little, Brown and Company is a division of Hachette Book Group, Inc. The Little, Brown name and logo are registered trademarks of Hachette Book Group, Inc. • The publisher is not responsible for websites (or their content) that are not owned by the publisher. • Little, Brown and Company books may be purchased in bulk for business, educational, or promotional use. For information, please contact your local bookseller or the Hachette Book Group Special Markets Department at special.markets@hbgusa.com. • Library of Congress Cataloging-in-Publication Data • Names: LaNier, Carlotta Walls, author. | Page, Lisa Frazier, author. | Brantley-Newton, Vanessa, illustrator. • Title: Carlotta's special dress / by Carlotta Walls LaNier with Lisa Frazier Page ; illustrated by Vanessa Brantley-Newton. • Description: New York : Little, Brown and Company, 2026. | Audience: Ages 6–8 | Summary: "The true story of Carlotta Walls LaNier's experience as one of the Little Rock Nine and the brand-new dress she bought in anticipation of her historic first day at an all-white school." —Provided by publisher. Identifiers: LCCN 2024019019 | ISBN 9780316572545 (hardcover) • Subjects: LCSH: LaNier, Carlotta Walls—Juvenile literature. | African American students—Arkansas—Little Rock—Biography—Juvenile literature. | Dresses—Social aspects—Arkansas—Little Rock—History—20th century—Juvenile literature. | Women's clothing—Social aspects—Arkansas—Little Rock—History—20th century—Juvenile literature. | School integration—Arkansas—Little Rock—History—20th century—Juvenile literature. | Central High School (Little Rock, Ark.)—History—Juvenile literature. • Classification: LCC LC214.23.L56 A3 2025 | DDC 379.2/630976773 [B]—dc23/eng/20240531 LC record available at https://lccn.loc.gov/2024019019 • ISBN 978-0-316-57254-5 • PRINTED IN DONGGUAN, CHINA • APS, 9/25 • 10 9 8 7 6 5 4 3 2 1

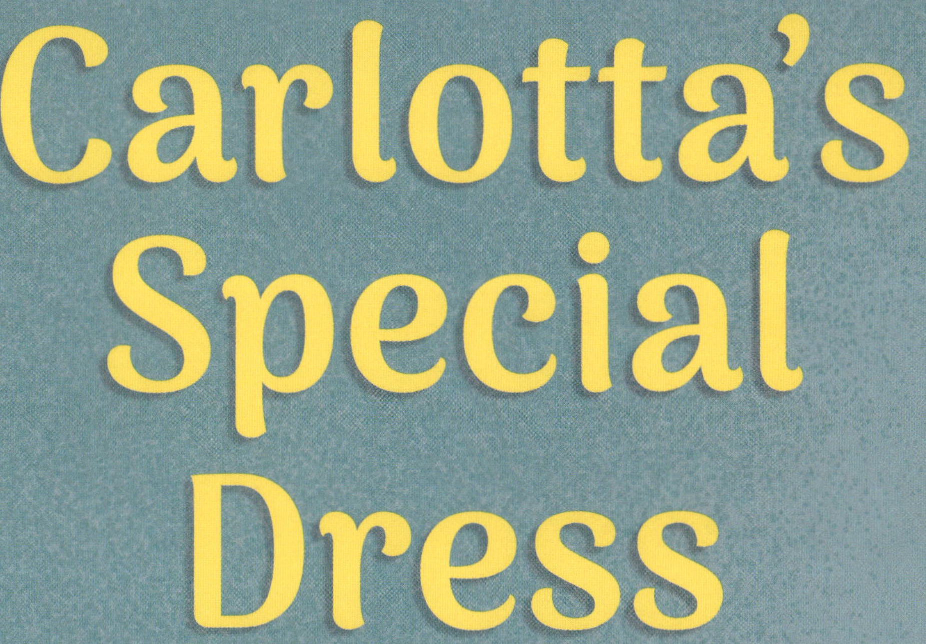

Carlotta's Special Dress

How a Walk to School Changed Civil Rights History

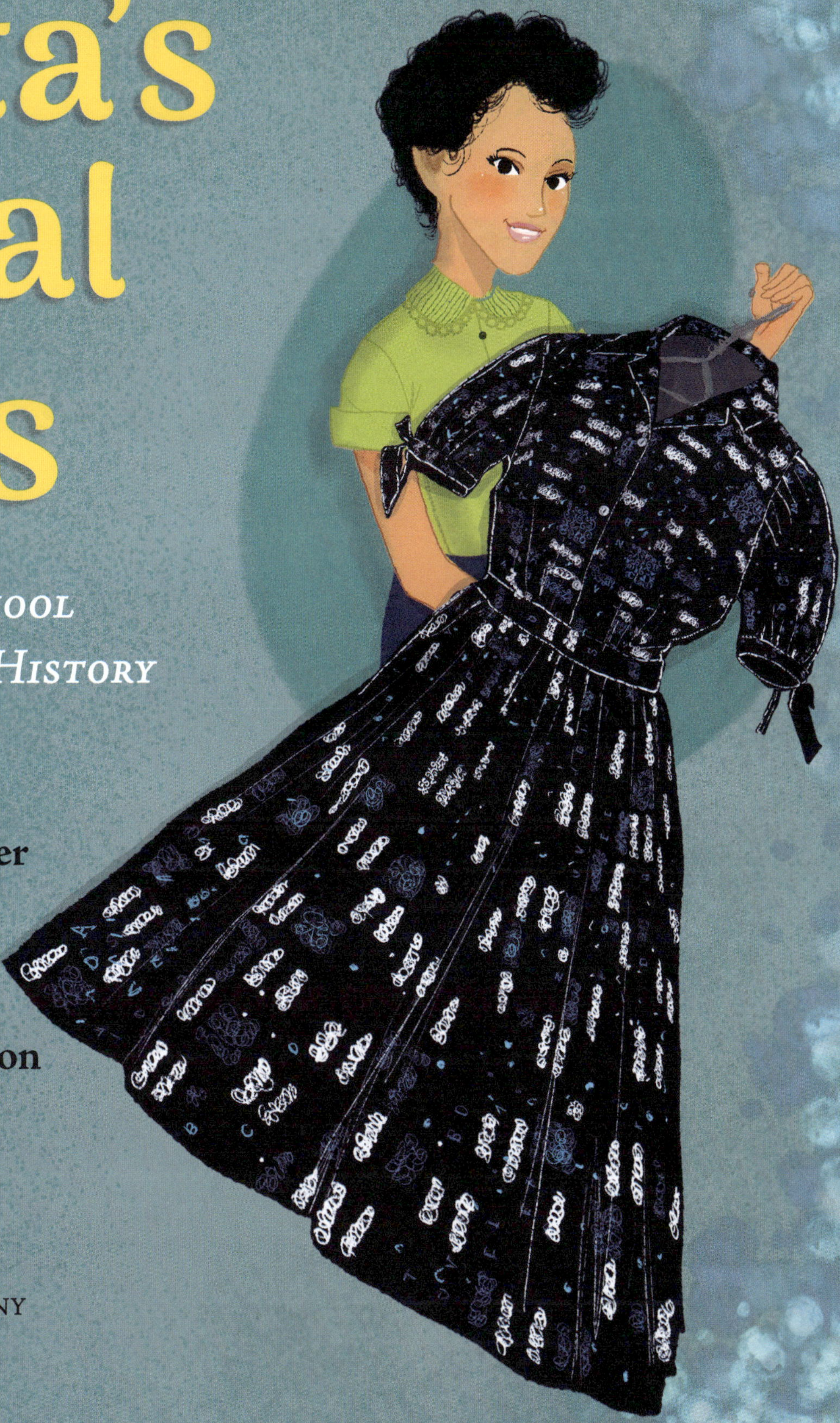

By Carlotta Walls LaNier
with Lisa Frazier Page

Illustrated by
Vanessa Brantley-Newton

LB 100 YEARS
LITTLE, BROWN AND COMPANY
New York Boston

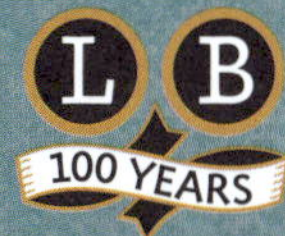

1957

Summer break is almost over, but I am the happiest girl in Little Rock because soon I'll be starting at my new school.

So when I answer a knock on our front door one sticky August day, I am all smiles. My favorite uncle, Emerald Holloway, waits for me on the other side.

"I have a surprise for you," Uncle Em says.

"What is it?" I ask excitedly.

He wraps me in a big bear hug and hands Mother a crisp twenty-dollar bill.

"Buy Carlotta a real nice dress," he says. "Everybody's going to be watching her first day at that school."

I rarely get a store-bought dress. Father works hard to provide for our family, so Mother saves money by making the clothes my two sisters and I wear every day. Sometimes, late at night, I can hear the whir of her old sewing machine making us something pretty. But Uncle Em is right. This will be a big day. I want to look perfect and make my family proud. I need to have a new dress.

McCall
PRINTED PATTERN

My new school, Central, is not just any school. It's one of the country's biggest, most beautiful schools. It sits just a mile from my house, and when we drive past, I stare out the window and wonder what it will be like to go there. I overhear adults say that Central is fancy inside and that it has a science lab with all the best equipment. I want to become a doctor someday, and that is just what I need to achieve my dreams.

For years, only white children could go to Central. But the laws have changed, and I will be one of the first Black students to attend.

After Uncle Em's visit, I lie awake listening to the radio. I am excited about going shopping with Mother for my special dress, but questions swirl in my mind, keeping me awake.

Will I like my new school?

How long will it take to learn my way around?

Will the other students want to be friends with me?

I remember kids love playing softball. I am pretty good at it. I stand taller than most, even the boys, so I am always one of the first players picked for a team. Maybe I'll get to play with the kids at my new school.

In my neighborhood, Black and white children live just blocks apart, so it seems strange that we have not been allowed to go to school together until now.

The next day, Mother and I ride the bus downtown to our favorite department store. But once inside, she heads straight for the frilly dresses.

"No ruffles or lace," I say, scrunching my nose.

Then she shows me one that is the color of her bright pink lipstick.

"Yuck!" I say, frowning. The color reminds me of tummy medicine.

Mother moves on, reaching for something with blue and white polka dots. I turn away so she can't see me roll my eyes. "No, no, no!"

Suddenly, I spot an outfit that I like. I dash to the rack and lift up the matching black skirt and blouse with small bluish-green letters and numbers all over.

The set is not too dainty. Or too bright. It's cute but simple enough to blend into the crowd without standing out or drawing much attention. It is exactly what I want.

The perfect dress for a perfect first day.

When the big day arrives, Mother wakes me up before my alarm clock. She has bad news: I won't be going to Central this morning.

Some white parents are angry that Black children and white children will attend school together in Little Rock. Mother says they are not open to change.

I am crushed. I cannot understand why those grown-ups don't want the best for all children. All I want are the same opportunities to learn that white children have.

Maybe when they see me in my special dress, they will see that I am not scary or bad. I'm just a girl with big dreams.

The next day, we learn that lawyers went to court to fight for our right to attend Central, and the judge sided with us. We can finally go to school!

I put on my new dress, and Mother drives me to meet the other Black students who will be attending Central. I know some of them from my old school, and we all quickly become friends. The plan is to walk to school together as a group, escorted by Black and white ministers who might put any crowds at ease.

Before we start walking, the ministers pray for everything to go smoothly. I pray that my new dress will bring good luck. We line up, with the white ministers in front, the students in the middle, and the Black ministers in the rear. It's time to make our way a few short blocks to Central.

As we get closer to the school, I hear shouting and chanting, like the sound of a crowd at a football game. But soon I see that this is not a happy crowd. People are angry and screaming at us in the distance! Who could be angry at children and ministers?

Some people yell for us to go home. Others shout mean things. My pretty new dress doesn't even matter. The crowd seems blinded by anger. My heart beats faster and faster, but I keep my head down and think about what my parents might say: *They're just mean people trying to scare you. Don't quit. Keep going.*

The next thing I know, we are standing in front of a line of soldiers in military uniforms. They form a ring around the school. Relief washes over me. They will protect us from the angry crowd.

But an officer tells one of the ministers that the Arkansas governor has ordered the National Guard to keep us out of Central.

"You should go on home," the officer says.

His words confuse me. Why does the governor want to keep children out of school? Isn't he supposed to follow the law?

Ernest, one of the boys in our group, bravely speaks up: "You're not going to let us in?"

The officer repeats his order for us to leave. The angry crowd yells in the background. My stomach tightens into a knot, but I refuse to cry. The ministers motion for us to turn around, and we have no choice but to walk away.

At home that evening, I turn on the television and see what happened on the news. But I do not want us to be on the news. I just want to go to school. Mother enters the living room, sits beside me, and takes my hand in hers. "Everything will be okay," she says. "We just have to wait a while longer."

Meanwhile, attorneys and important civil rights leaders come to Little Rock to help fight the governor's order in court. Nine students are planning to attend Central: Ernest, Terrence, Jefferson, Melba, Gloria, Minnijean, Elizabeth, Thelma, and me. Some of them didn't make it to the meeting spot the first day and tried to make it to school on their own.

Reporters say we are pioneers. Eventually, they start calling us the Little Rock Nine.

Nearly three weeks after our first attempt to go to school, we try again and even make it inside Central. But the crowd outside grows bigger and scarier, and we are quickly taken from our classes to the basement, then whisked away in a police car.

"Don't stop for anything," an officer says to the driver as we speed away from the school.

The news has been reporting about the dangerous crowd all morning, and Mother is waiting for me at our front door. Her face is as pale as a sheet of paper, and her eyes are red and puffy. She throws her arms around me, and Father does, too, when he makes it home. "Are you okay?" Mother asks again and again.

I pull away and drag myself to my room. Maybe I will never see that amazing science lab or achieve my dream of becoming a doctor. Maybe my special dress isn't so special after all. Without a word, I pack it away. I never want to wear it again.

Uncle Em calls to check on me. "Don't lose hope," he says. His words remind me of our family's quiet strength. We don't give up easily.

The news about Little Rock makes it to President Dwight Eisenhower, and the next night, my family watches as he announces on television that he is sending us help. "For a few minutes this evening, I should like to speak to you about the serious situation that has arisen in Little Rock," he says.

He has sent a special unit of the US Army known as the Screaming Eagles, the 101st Airborne, to protect us and force the adults to obey the law.

I can't believe it! The president of the United States is talking about us! I am so excited.

The next morning, I wake up with the sun. Finally, I am going to school!

I think about putting on my special dress. But it reminds me of screaming, anger, and hate. After so much bad luck, I don't want to take any chances.

By eight o'clock that morning, all nine of us are gathered at the home of Mrs. Daisy Bates, who is the state leader of the National Association for the Advancement of Colored People.

Suddenly, we hear a loud rumble outside. Soldiers dressed in military uniforms and helmets jump out of topless Jeeps and form a line.

The Screaming Eagles have come to keep us safe.

This time, the angry crowds are smaller and quieter as the military station wagon drives us to the front of Central.

We line up mostly in pairs, surrounded by soldiers. Slowly, we begin to move together up a long walkway. I have seen the tall stairs leading into Central many times before. But walking them today feels like climbing the highest mountain. Everyone is silent.

When we make it to the top, I sigh with relief and step past the heavy wooden front doors. Pride rises inside me. Pride in my country for defending us. Pride in my parents for strength and guidance. And pride in the nine of us for never giving up. Now, in this special moment, the world is watching us win.

And maybe someday, somehow, the dress I packed away will feel special again too.

Carlotta LaNier and
Central High School

AUTHOR'S NOTE

My hope for the special dress I packed away one frustrating day in 1957 did come true—fifty-five years later! In 2012, I donated it to the Smithsonian's National Museum of African American History and Culture. By then, the country had changed, and my eight comrades and I, still called the Little Rock Nine, had become celebrated as pioneers in this country's battle to desegregate public schools.

President Dwight Eisenhower's decision to send the US Army's elite 101st Airborne Division to escort us into Central High School on September 25, 1957, was historic. It marked the first time a US president dispatched the army to enforce a federal school desegregation order. (The US Supreme Court had decided three years earlier that separating children in schools based on their race was unconstitutional.)

In May 1955, Little Rock school officials developed a plan to phase in integration slowly, beginning with Central. Central was a grand, beautiful school that spread across four square blocks just a mile from my house. It had a stellar academic reputation and state-of-the-art equipment. I dreamed of becoming a doctor and believed Central would put me on that path. So, when my ninth-grade teacher announced that Central would be integrating in 1957, I signed a sheet that he was passing around for interested Black students who lived in the attendance zone.

I didn't realize until decades later that the decision to attend Central was not mine alone. School officials thoroughly scrutinized every Black student who expressed interest and selected those of us who were on the honor roll, active in extracurricular activities, and from stable families. About thirty-nine of us and our parents showed up for a special mandatory meeting with Superintendent Virgil T. Blossom in his office. Most of the students surely lost interest when Blossom went over the rules, the most disappointing of which was that we would have to leave school grounds immediately after classes ended. Black students were not allowed to participate in any extracurricular activities. No school dances. No clubs. No sports.

I just figured it all would be temporary. Even during the summer, as opposition from white residents to the school system's integration plans began to grow, I paid little attention. My excitement about attending Central only grew when my great-uncle Emerald Holloway surprised me with the money to get that brand-new dress for my first day.

On September 4, 1957, after a federal court ordered the school system to proceed with its integration plans, we made our way to Central and faced an angry white mob. But the Arkansas National Guard turned us away from the school, and one of the students, Jane Hill, never returned. Another student, Elizabeth Eckford, did not get the message that we were to meet a few blocks away from Central and walk together as a group escorted by ministers. Elizabeth tried to enter the school alone and was followed and taunted by the mob. Two other students, Melba Pattillo and Terrence Roberts, also walked to school separately that day but were turned away.

With the city of Little Rock in chaos a couple of weeks later, President Eisenhower finally intervened. But getting inside Central was just half the battle. Even though each Black student had a military escort at Central that year, white students still spit on us, called us derogatory names, left nasty notes on our lockers, and kicked and hit us. One girl with bright red hair regularly walked on my heels until they bled. We had been warned that we would get in trouble if we fought back, but one of us, Minnijean Brown, did just that when a group of boys kept calling her names and blocked her path in the school cafeteria. She dropped her bowl of chili on one boy's head and was expelled from school. The NAACP arranged for her to finish the school year in New York.

The remaining eight of us—Gloria Ray, Jefferson Thomas, Thelma Mothershed, Melba, Terrence, Elizabeth, Ernest, and I—made it through that school year. Ernest, the oldest, became the first Black graduate of Central.

The next school year, Arkansas Governor Orval Faubus closed all four public high schools in Little Rock to avoid further integration. The move hurt students of all races, who were suddenly forced to take correspondence courses or move out of town to attend school. When Little Rock high schools reopened the following year, I returned to Central as a senior. In May 1960, I became the first female Black student to participate in a graduation ceremony at the school. The next morning, I boarded a train and left Little Rock for good.

I briefly attended Michigan State University, but the lost year of schooling in Little Rock prevented me from taking the rigorous math and science courses I needed to be successful in the university's premed program. I left Michigan State and went to live with relatives in Denver, where my parents and sisters soon joined me. I never became a medical doctor, but I ultimately finished college at Colorado State College (now the University of Northern Colorado), got married, had a son and a daughter, and founded my own real estate brokerage firm. I have been awarded six honorary doctorate degrees, and in November 1999, President Bill Clinton and the US Congress presented each member of the Little Rock Nine with the Congressional Gold Medal, the highest civilian award bestowed by Congress.

TIMELINE

May 17, 1954

The US Supreme Court decides that segregated schools are unconstitutional in the case *Brown v. Board of Education*.

May 24, 1955

The Little Rock School District decides integrating Central in 1957 will be its first step. The integration plan becomes known as the Blossom Plan, after Superintendent Virgil T. Blossom.

May 31, 1955

The US Supreme Court officially orders school systems to begin making plans to integrate schools. The court says integration should happen "with all deliberate speed."

September 2, 1957

Arkansas Governor Orval Faubus announces on television that he has sent the Arkansas National Guard to keep things peaceful at Central.

September 3, 1957

Black students miss the first day of school after Superintendent Blossom instructs them to stay home. Classes still go on for white students.

September 4, 1957

The Arkansas National Guard prevents the Black students from entering Central. The ordeal is shown on television that night.

September 20, 1957

US District Judge Ronald Davies rules that Governor Faubus can no longer block the Black students from attending Central.

September 23, 1957

The Little Rock Nine make it into Central and go to classes, but the angry crowd outside grows violent. At noon, the Black students are rushed home for their safety. Little Rock Mayor Woodrow Wilson Mann sends a telegram to President Dwight Eisenhower, informing him of the situation at Central.

September 24, 1957

Mayor Mann sends a second telegram to President Eisenhower, pleading for his help controlling the dangerous situation. Eisenhower orders federal troops to Little Rock and announces his decision on television that night.

September 25, 1957

The Little Rock Nine are escorted into Central by members of the US Army's 101st Airborne Division, also known as the Screaming Eagles.

May 27, 1958

Ernest Green becomes the first Black student to graduate from Central.

September 12, 1958

Governor Faubus closes all Little Rock public high schools rather than allow integration to continue. Carlotta, with the help of the NAACP, takes correspondence courses and, in April 1959, moves to Cleveland to finish the school year. She then moves to Chicago to stay with relatives for summer school. Little Rock schools remain closed for a year.

May 30, 1960

Carlotta graduates from Central.

May 31, 1960

Carlotta leaves Little Rock. She never again returns to live.

September 27, 2012

Carlotta donates her special dress to the Smithsonian's National Museum of African American History and Culture.

My mother, Juanita Walls, reminds me of an elegant movie star in this 1950s photo.

My father, Cartelyou Walls, looking handsome in the 1950s. I was a daddy's girl growing up.

I am about four years old here with my mother and father at our home in Little Rock.

I recall not liking the long ponytails I wore in elementary school, so I got my hair cut short in high school. I have kept it short ever since.

I listen in shock on September 4, 1957, as the commander of the Arkansas National Guard tells a group of us that his troops are under orders from the governor to keep Black students out of Central. To my left are Gloria Ray and Ernest Green, and standing behind Gloria is Jane Hill. Jane never returned after that first attempt to enter Central.

Elizabeth Eckford is taunted as she tries to make her way to Central alone on September 4, 1957.

My parents are all smiles at a friend's house in 1961 in Kansas City, Missouri, where they moved after leaving Little Rock for good.

I exit a government station wagon on September 25, 1957, after President Eisenhower sends the 101st Airborne Division to escort us—the Little Rock Nine—into Central. Minnijean Brown steps out behind me.

My mother and I together at an event in the mid-2000s.